Saudi Arabia

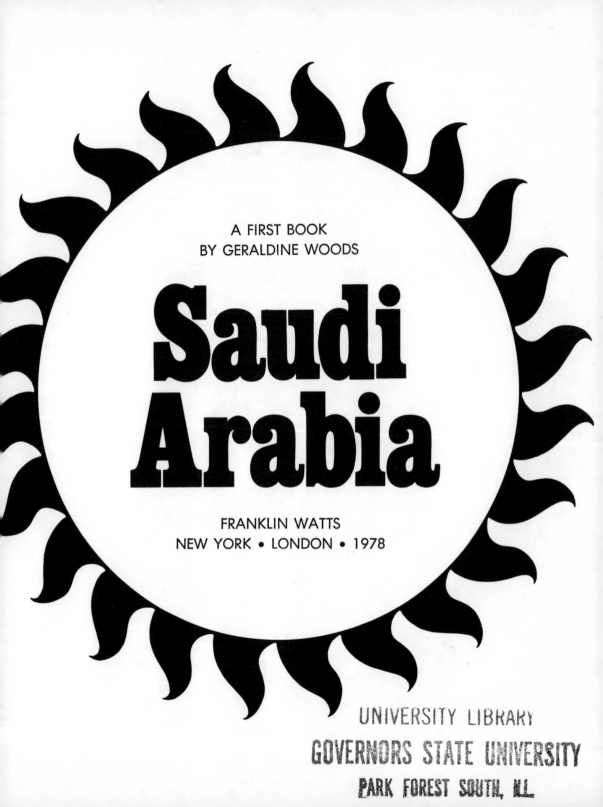

A FIRST BOOK
BY GERALDINE WOODS

Saudi Arabia

FRANKLIN WATTS
NEW YORK • LONDON • 1978

Cover design by Jackie Schuman

Photographs courtesy of:
United Arab Emirates: p. 8; Aramco: pp. 13 (Bur-
nett. H. Moody), 26, 52; Arab Information Cen-
ter: pp. 14, 17; Leo deWys, Inc.: pp. 20, 45, 48;
United Press International: pp. 30, 40, 49; UN/
World Health Organization: p. 33.

Maps courtesy of: Vantage Art, Inc.

Library of Congress Cataloging in Publication Data

Woods, Geraldine.
    Saudi Arabia.

    (A First book)
    Bibliography: p.
    Includes index.
    SUMMARY: Discusses the history, geogra-
phy, people and culture of Saudi Arabia and its
evolvement during the past 50 years from a poor
backward country to one of the wealthiest in the
world.
    1. Saudi Arabia—Juvenile literature. [1.
Saudi Arabia] I. Title.
DS204.W66   953'.8'05   78-9517
ISBN 0-531-02234-X

Contents

Saudi Arabia

Saudi Arabia: A Land of Hidden Treasure

There is an old Arabian story about a poor man named Ali Baba. One day he saw what looked to him like an ordinary mountain. A strange man went up to the mountain, said some magic words, and to Ali Baba's surprise, the mountain opened. Inside the mountain Ali saw vast treasures — gold, silver, and precious stones. After some exciting adventures, Ali Baba took possession of the treasure. He used it wisely and it made him, his children, and his children's children very rich people.

The story of Ali Baba is a little like the story of the Kingdom of Saudi Arabia. Like Ali Baba, Saudi Arabia was once very poor. Because it is one of the hottest and driest countries in the world, little food can be grown and few animals can be raised there.

(1)

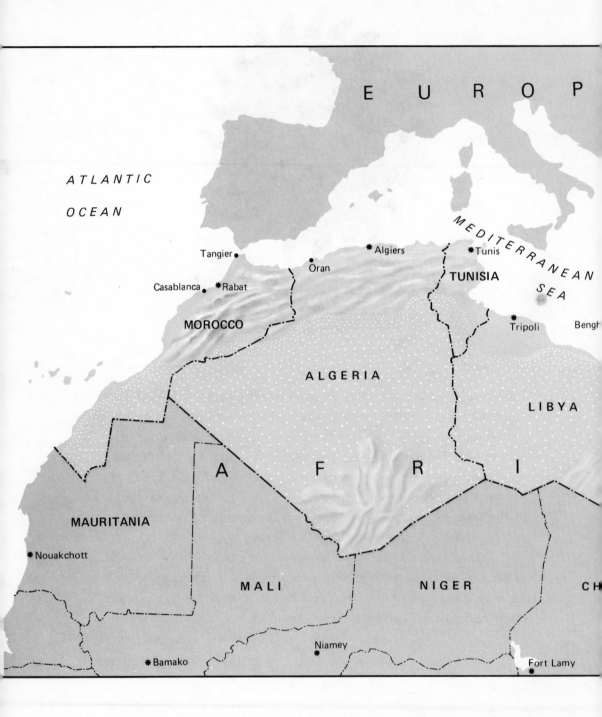

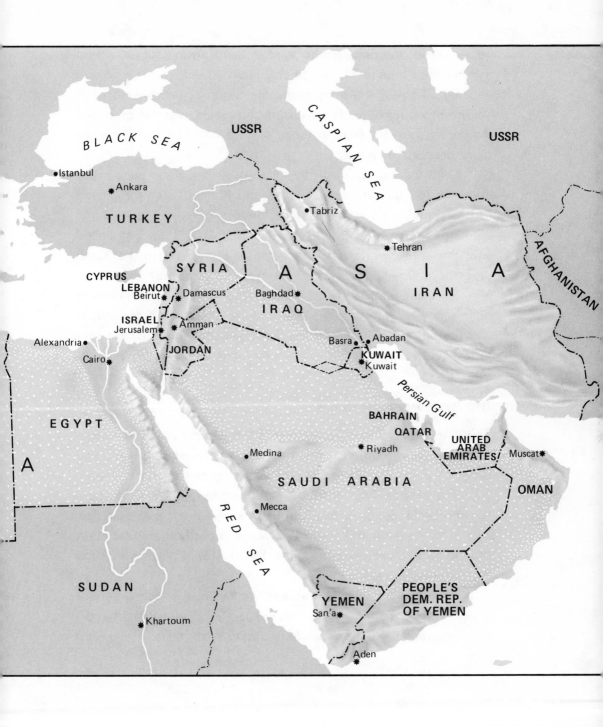

For centuries, the people who lived in Saudi Arabia had to spend most of their time just trying to stay alive.

But like Ali Baba's mountain, the desert of Saudi Arabia hid an enormous treasure. This treasure, however, was not gold and diamonds, but oil. And in today's industrial world, oil is even more precious than gold.

Oil is the fuel that runs the modern world. Some oil is made into fuel, to run cars, trucks, boats, and planes. Some oil is used to heat homes. Oil also runs machines that make electricity to light our houses and power our factories. In this industrialized age, the entire world needs energy, and underneath the Saudi desert is a huge supply of that energy, in the form of oil.

So, like Ali Baba, Saudi Arabia became very rich. Billions of dollars flowed into this desert kingdom, changing it forever. It was the hot and sandy land that kept Saudi Arabia poor for centuries; and it was the land that finally made Saudi Arabia rich.

THE ARABIAN PENINSULA

Saudi Arabia is located in the part of the world called the Middle East. Europeans named it this because it seemed about midway between Europe and the Far East countries of China and Japan.

The Middle East is in the southwestern part of the continent of Asia. Saudi Arabia itself is in an area of the Middle East known as the Arabian Peninsula, a large, roughly triangular piece of land with water on three sides. Saudi Arabia fills most of the Arabian Peninsula.

To the west of Saudi Arabia is the Red Sea, which separates it from Egypt. To the east is the Persian Gulf, which the Saudis call the Arabian Gulf. The ancient kingdom of Persia, now called

(4)

Iran, is across the Persian Gulf. Ringing Saudi Arabia on the south and east are several small countries — Yemen, the People's Democratic Republic of Yemen, Oman, the United Arab Emirates, and Qatar. To the north of Saudi Arabia are Jordan, Iraq, and Kuwait.

THE WEATHER

Saudi Arabia is large in land area and small in population. It has an area of about 830,000 square miles (2,150,000 sq km), yet only seven million people live there. Undoubtedly one reason so few people live in Saudi Arabia is that it is such a difficult place to live. Most of the country is desert, with some of the hottest and driest weather on earth.

When the Saudi Arabians say it is hot outside, they mean it. The average temperature is 90° F (32° C), but it is often as hot as 120° F (49° C) or more. Once, in the southern desert, the temperature reached 165° F (74° C). Average temperatures are a little lower in winter. A Saudi who lives in the desert also has to get used to great changes of temperature daily. As soon as the sun goes down the temperature falls rapidly, sometimes going as low as freezing. It could be 100° F (38° C) during the day and 40° F (4° C) at night.

The intense heat affects every part of Saudi life, even the language. When something makes us feel good, we call it "heart-warming." The Saudis, however, call it "heart-cooling"!

Saudi Arabia is also one of the driest countries in the world. The Western Highlands get the most rain, but even that is only 12 to 20 inches (30 to 50 cm) a year. The average yearly rainfall for the whole country is only 4 inches (10 cm), and in some parts of Saudi Arabia it doesn't rain for 10 years at a time. Because there is so little rain, there are no rivers or lakes in the entire country. But there are bridges that cross *wadis,* or dry valleys, which fill up with water after rainstorms. These small streams don't last long, however, because the desert heat soon dries them up.

THE LAND

Although Saudi Arabia is largely desert, there are other land regions as well. Near the Persian Gulf are the Eastern Lowlands, where most of the oil deposits have been found so far. This region is hot and humid and often covered by dense fogs. The land is flat and sandy, with some marshes.

Along the Red Sea is a narrow, flat plain. West of this plain are mountains that extend almost the whole length of the country. They are called Hejaz in the north and Asir in the south. The mountainous areas of the south have enough rain to grow several types of crops.

In the middle of the country is a high, flat plateau, forming a dry and rocky area. The capital city of Riyadh is located in this central plateau.

The northern and southern parts of the country are deserts, and form the hottest and driest parts of the country. The southern desert is the largest. Saudi Arabians call it Rub' al-Khali, which means "empty quarter" and that's exactly what it is. Very few people, animals, or plants live there. The sand is many-hued — red, gold, silver, purple, and brown — and is blown by the wind into enormous hills called dunes that sometimes reach a height of 600 feet (183 m) and stretch over 10 miles (16 km). The months of May, June, and July bring the sandstorm season, when

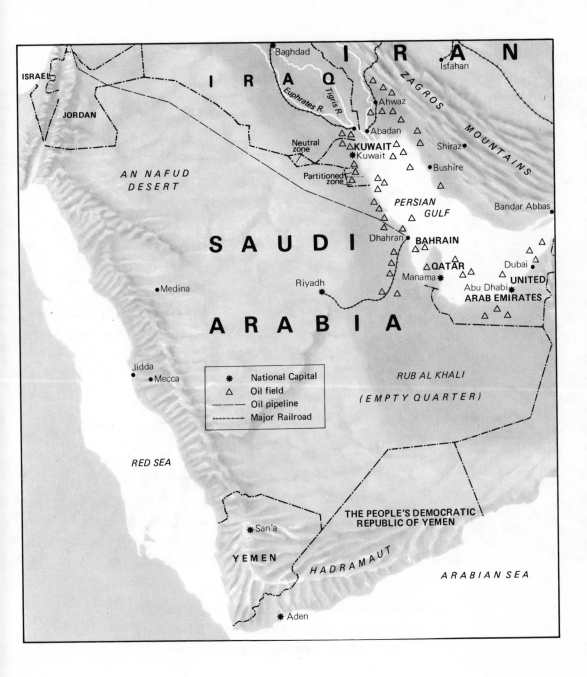

ISRAEL

JORDAN

I R A Q

Baghdad

I R A N

Isfahan

Euphrates R.

Tigris R.

Ahwaz

ZAGROS

Abadan

Neutral
zone

KUWAIT

Kuwait

Shiraz

MOUNTAINS

Partitioned
zone

Bushire

AN NAFUD
DESERT

PERSIAN
GULF

Bandar Abbas

Dhahran

BAHRAIN

S A U D I

QATAR

Dubai

Manama

UNITED

Medina

Riyadh

Abu Dhabi

ARAB EMIRATES

A R A B I A

Jidda

Mecca

RUB AL KHALI

(EMPTY QUARTER)

✳ National Capital

△ Oil field

—·— Oil pipeline

++++ Major Railroad

RED SEA

THE PEOPLE'S DEMOCRATIC
REPUBLIC OF YEMEN

✳ San'a

YEMEN

HADRAMAUT

ARABIAN SEA

✳ Aden

Saudi Arabia is one of the hottest, driest countries
in the world. In fact, some parts of the country
don't get any rainfall for years at a time.

strong winds pick up the sand and swirl it about. The air becomes thick with dust, making it difficult to see or even breathe.

OASES IN THE DESERT

The climate and land of Saudi Arabia are not easy to live with. Fortunately, there is some relief in the form of underground springs that provide water for people, animals, and plants. Wherever these underground springs come to the surface a small area of green brightens the desert landscape. These places are called oases and the people of Saudi Arabia could not live without them. Oases can be very small, with no more than a couple of palm trees, or they can be quite large, with many houses, animals, and farmland dependent on their water. Some of Saudi Arabia's major cities, including the capital, Riyadh, are built on oases. Oases are now being made artificially, through irrigation.

"SHIPS OF THE DESERT"

A valuable talent in the desert is the ability to survive with very little water. For this reason the camel is the most important animal in Saudi Arabia. Camels can go several days without drinking because they have the ability to store about 30 gallons (136 l) of water in their bodies.

Camels have other abilities that help them live in the desert. During sandstorms, they can close their nostrils to small slits, in order to keep sand out of their noses. They also have long, thick eyelashes to protect their eyes from sand in the air.

Camels help the people who live in the desert in many ways. Their milk is a nourishing drink, and their hair can be made into tents and clothing. They are a good means of transportation.

They are sometimes even used as money. They are so important that there are over a thousand words for camel in Arabic, the Saudi Arabian language.

Another important animal in Saudi Arabia is the Arabian horse, famous for its speed and beauty. Many race horses are descended from Arabian stock. But since they require a lot of water, horses in Saudi Arabia are a luxury, and only the rich can afford to own them.

Antelopes, foxes, wolves, leopards, and wildcats are some of the many other animals that live in Saudi Arabia.

PLANT LIFE

Many people picture deserts as large stretches of land with no trees or plants. Fortunately for the Saudis, that's not the case. In spite of the dry climate, many plants grow in Saudi Arabia.

In the oases, there is enough water to grow food crops, especially dates. Grown on tall date palm trees, dates are a very popular fruit. They can be eaten as fruit, baked into cakes, or made into a drink, and their pits provide food for camels. Grapes, almonds, and sugar cane are some other crops grown on oases.

Surprisingly, many plants grow wild in the desert. Some, like cactus, can store water to get them through the dry periods. Since plants lose water through their leaves, many types of cactus and other desert plants have small, needlelike leaves. This reduces the amount of moisture lost to the sun.

There are even some wildflowers in the desert. *Zahra hamra* is a plant with pink flowers that blooms in March and April. There are also many types of bushes growing in Saudi Arabia. One of these, the *rak*, is used by desert-dwellers as a toothbrush. Bushes are also an important food source for camels.

The People

Saudi Arabia wasn't always such a dry land. About 25,000 years ago there was enough rain to make the land green with growing plants. Temperatures were lower, and there were forests, lakes, and seas.

But very slowly the climate began to change, and over a period of 10,000 years the land became hotter and drier. Finally, Saudi Arabia became the desert it is today.

Sometime during those years human beings began to live in the Arabian Peninsula. No one knows exactly when they came, but they had definitely arrived by the year 15,000 B.C. But as the Arabian climate changed, many people moved away. They went to the north or toward the sea, looking for water and cooler weather. Those who stayed on the Arabian Peninsula became known as Semites because of the legend that says they were descended from a man called Shem. Shem is named in the Bible as the oldest son of Noah. Hebrews, or Jews, are also Semites. Today, most of the seven million people who live in Saudi Arabia are descendants of the original Semites who settled there thousands of years ago.

BEDOUINS:
A WANDERING PEOPLE

Some of the people who stayed in Arabia as it became a desert settled in oases. There they built villages and towns. They planted date palms and other crops to feed themselves. But others, called Bedouins, stayed in the desert. The only way the Bedouins could survive in the desert was by developing a new way of life.

The Bedouins couldn't settle in the oases because the goats and sheep they raised needed grass to eat. In a country with lots of rain, grass grows back quickly after animals graze on it. But in the desert it takes a long time for grass to grow again, so the desert people had to move on every time the grass ran out in one place. The Bedouins had to keep wandering, always looking for food for their animals.

After a while this wandering became a way of life, and the Bedouin tribes learned how to live without a permanent home. The Bedouins, and all the people who live a life of wandering, are called nomads. Although there are not as many as there used to be, many people in Saudi Arabia are still nomads. Their way of life has changed a little since the discovery of oil, but for the most part the Bedouins follow traditions that are centuries old.

A Bedouin man and his son. While their lifestyle has changed some since the discovery of oil in Saudi Arabia, most Bedouins still follow traditions that are centuries old.

Water is now piped in to some remote desert areas
for both Bedouins and their animals.
Note the camel-hair tents in the background.

DESERT LIFE

A stranger who tried to live in the desert would probably not survive for very long. But through the years the Bedouins have learned everything there is to know about their environment. They have created a way of life that is perfect for their desert home.

Since they are always on the move, the Bedouins can't build houses. Instead they live in tents made of black camel's hair. They have few possessions because everything they own has to be carried with them on their travels.

The most important possessions owned by the Bedouins are their animals. Their camels provide them with milk and food, and can be traded for things the tribe needs. In the past, they were the Bedouins' only means of transportation. Today, however, some Bedouins use modern trucks to get around.

Goats and sheep are raised for food, and extra animals are traded when the tribe stops at an oasis. The people in the oasis exchange vegetables and fruit for meat from the goats and sheep.

Bedouin clothing is perfectly suited for life in the desert. Instead of pants and a shirt, a Bedouin man wears a long, loose robe. This is cooler because more air can circulate around his body and he can take advantage of every breeze. To protect his head from the hot desert sun, a Bedouin wears a flowing head-dress, kept in place by a black cord that is wrapped twice around his head. The Bedouin's robe is usually white. His head cloth is either all white or patterned with red and white checks. A sleeveless brown coat made of camel's hair warms him on cold desert nights. A Bedouin woman wears a long, loose dress, often covered by a long black cloak. Both men and women usually go barefoot in the desert.

(15)

Bedouins are experts at living in the desert. They can find their way around as well as city-dwellers can in their own town. The Bedouins know the sand so well that they can tell the height and weight of a person from his or her footprint in the sand. A Bedouin's description of a footprint is accepted as evidence in Saudi Arabian courts, the same way fingerprints are accepted in ours.

Bedouins are very proud of their families and loyal to their tribes. Any person who is lost in the desert or in need of help is taken in as one of the family. Any food or water the tribe has, no matter how little, will be shared with the stranger. But they have a very strict code of conduct. If anyone hurts a member of the tribe, the Bedouins will quickly seek revenge. In recent years the national government has taken over the job of law enforcement. In some places, however, the rule is still, "An eye for an eye, a tooth for a tooth."

Since the discovery of oil in Saudi Arabia, many Bedouins are giving up their nomadic way of life and moving into the cities. The government trains them for new jobs or teaches them how to farm on oases. But many Bedouins are still content to stay in the desert. It is a difficult life, but they like it.

LIVING ON AN OASIS

The nomad's way of life would seem strange to most people. Living on an oasis, on the other hand, is very much like living in any small town. A village on an oasis has farmland, houses, a church, and a place to buy and sell things.

In the middle of a typical Saudi village is the suq, an outdoor marketplace. People gather at the suq to buy and sell all kinds of things. Food, animals, rugs, household goods, clothing —

Bedouins bring their sheep and other merchandise to sell and trade at an open-air marketplace in Hofuf, an oasis city.

everything can be found at the suq. But there is more to the suq than buying and selling. People come to visit, talk, and see friends. It is one of the liveliest places in the village.

Another important spot is the *ain*, or the village well. Some larger towns in Saudi Arabia have been modernized and have running water in each house. But the smaller villages still rely on the ain as their only source of water, and people come to the ain to get the water they need for their homes.

Also in the middle of town is the village church. Saudi Arabians belong to the Muslim religion, and their church is called a mosque. From this church, five times a day, an official of the church calls the people to prayer.

If the town is large enough, it will also have some coffee shops, or cafés. Saudi Arabian men like to meet over a cup of coffee and discuss the events of the day with their friends.

In addition to these public places, the village also has many private homes. Most of these are made of mud brick and are built in a hollow square pattern. The middle of the square is an open courtyard, often with a fountain in the middle. The sides of the square are rooms where the family lives. Most Saudi houses also have a small garden.

The village is surrounded by orchards, farmland, and fields for animals to graze in. Some of the older villages have mud brick walls around them that were built long ago as a protection against raids by unfriendly tribes.

Most of the people who live in the oases are farmers. Some others make their living as traders, buying and selling all kinds of goods. The villagers' clothes are very much like the Bedouins'. In town, however, people usually wear sandals or other types of shoes instead of going barefoot.

History

Before Saudi Arabia was established as a nation in 1932, the Arabian Peninsula was controlled by a number of tribes. Each tribe was ruled by a sheikh, an official chosen by the tribesmen because they thought he was an able leader. He remained sheikh only as long as the tribe thought he was doing a good job. After that, he was replaced by someone else.

Because they lived in the middle of several important trade routes, trading became an important industry of early Bedouin tribes. The kingdoms to the north and west — Syria, Mesopotamia (now Iraq), and Egypt — traded with Yemen, a country located at the southern end of the Arabian Peninsula. Other countries in Asia, such as India, traded with Africa and the kingdoms of the Middle East. All these trade routes passed

Mecca, the birthplace of Mohammed, as it looks today.

through the Arabian Peninsula. Since the Bedouins were experts at moving through the desert, they soon developed a profitable business. They transported silks, spices, ivory, animal skins, and many other things back and forth between these nations. The goods were carried across the desert by camels, usually moving in groups called caravans. Other Arabians traded by ship on the Red Sea and the Persian Gulf.

A NEW FAITH

Cities grew up along the major trade routes to provide food and shelter for the caravans. One of these was Mecca, located in the hilly western area of Saudi Arabia. It was in the city of Mecca that a child named Mohammed was born, around the year 570 A.D. His birth changed forever the history of the Arabian Peninsula. In fact, it could even be said that Mohammed changed the history of the whole world.

Little is known about Mohammed's early life. We do know that at the age of 25 he married a widow named Kadijah. At the time of his marriage, Mecca was a rough city, with no organized government. Groups of families called clans fought with each other all the time. The people worshipped many gods, and many people were poor.

Mohammed began to go off into the hills outside Mecca to think and pray. One day he came back and told Kadijah that he had received a message from the Angel Gabriel. The message was simple: "There is only one God. He is all-powerful. He created the whole universe. People should obey Him."

Some of the people accepted Mohammed's message right away. They formed a new religion which was called Islam. People who believed in this religion were called Muslims.

(21)

But not everyone in Mecca accepted the new faith. Mohammed and his followers were often persecuted for their beliefs. To escape this persecution Mohammed fled to the nearby city of Medina in the year 622. In Medina the Muslims were welcomed, and their new religion grew stronger and spread to other towns. Mohammed was accepted by more and more people as a messenger from God. In towns where most people were Muslims, Mohammed became both head of the church and head of the government. Since one of Mohammed's teachings was that all Muslims were brothers, fighting between members of the church stopped.

THE EMPIRE

Fighting with non-Muslims, on the other hand, increased. One of Mohammed's teachings was that people who died for their faith would go straight to heaven. Since they had no fear of death, Muslim soldiers were brave and fierce fighters. They wanted to conquer new lands and place them under Muslim rule. By the year 630, Mohammed was able to recapture Mecca. When he died in the year 632, all of the Arabian Peninsula was controlled by Muslims.

Mohammed's successors expanded their empire still further. By the year 750, Muslim soldiers had conquered Egypt, Northern Africa, Spain, parts of France, most of the Middle East, and parts of Afghanistan and India. Many of the conquered people converted to Islam, although other faiths were allowed. The language and culture of the Arabian Peninsula were also brought to the conquered lands. The people of the Arabian Empire became known as Arabs.

At the height of the Empire, there were many advances in

science and learning, including important discoveries in chemistry and astronomy. The English word *chemistry*, for example, comes from the Arabic word *al-kimiya*. Many stars were named by Arabs, such as *Altair* (the Eagle) and *Algedi* (the Goat). Great progress was also made in mathematics and medicine.

But at the same time that the Empire was growing, some things were happening that would eventually cause it to fall apart. The Crusades, for example, damaged the Empire. These were a series of wars that took place from the eleventh to the thirteenth centuries. They were fought with the European Christians, who wanted to regain control over the land where Christ had lived. The Christians lost these wars, but the Arabian Empire was weakened all the same.

Within the Empire there were other troubles. When Mohammed died, there were struggles for power among his followers. The government did not always rule honestly, and money was wasted. Communication between the ruler and distant parts of the Empire was difficult. Gradually, some conquered peoples won back their land. Other nations, such as Turkey, captured territory from the Arabian Empire. By the end of the sixteenth century, the Arabian Empire had completely fallen apart.

Most of the people who had been part of the Arabian Empire kept the same culture and religion. Even today, the people of these countries speak and write Arabic. The countries of the Arabian Empire are no longer united politically, but they still share a common bond — they are all Arabs.

IBN SAUD

After the Arabian Empire fell, the Peninsula had a number of rulers. Turkey controlled parts of the center and northwest. In the nineteenth century, Great Britain established colonies on the southern and eastern coasts. Most of the middle of the Peninsula was ruled by Bedouin tribes.

One of these tribes was governed by a family named Saud. The Saud family had held power for a short time in the nineteenth century. In 1902, a member of the family named Ibn Saud captured the city of Riyadh. During the next 25 years, Ibn Saud won more and more territory, so that by 1926 most of Arabia was united under his rule. In 1932 the country received its official name: the Kingdom of Saudi Arabia.

Ibn Saud ruled for 20 more years. When he died in 1953, his son Saud became king. But Saud was a poor money-manager, and in 1960 he gave control of the government to his brother Faisal for two years. Faisal was such a good ruler that the kingship was given to him permanently in 1964. In March, 1975, Faisal was assassinated. His half-brother Khalid then became king.

OIL

When King Ibn Saud unified his country in 1932, Saudi Arabia was still very poor. But during his reign oil was discovered in the eastern district. It made Saudi Arabia one of the richest countries in the world.

Hundreds of millions of years ago, the Persian Gulf was much larger than it is today. Much of Saudi Arabia's eastern coast was under water. Throughout the centuries, the plants and animals that lived in the Gulf died, and their bodies drifted to the ocean floor. Slowly, the bodies of these ancient living things were changed into oil.

The Bedouins who journeyed over the desert sand didn't realize that they were walking on top of a priceless treasure. But scientists who worked for an American oil company suspected there might be oil there. King Ibn Saud asked the Bedouins to help these scientists as they looked for oil. In 1933, the first discovery was made. Many more discoveries followed. Soon it was clear that one of the largest deposits of oil ever found was in the Kingdom of Saudi Arabia. Today, Saudi Arabia has the most extensive oil reserves and exports the largest amount of oil of any country in the world.

Several American oil companies went into partnership with the Saudis. They formed a company called the Arabian-American Oil Company (ARAMCO for short). At first the Saudis got only a small part of the money from the sale of their oil. But even that was enough to make them rich. As time went on, the Saudis took more and more control over ARAMCO, and received a bigger share of the profits.

The Saudis also joined with other oil countries in 1960 to form OPEC, the Organization of Petroleum Exporting Countries. Thirteen nations that depend on oil exports for their money are members of OPEC. Each member nation is stronger because all the countries of OPEC usually agree to make the same decisions. In 1974, for example, Saudi Arabia decided to raise the price of oil sold to other nations. The other OPEC countries did the same, so that countries buying oil from any of the OPEC countries had no choice but to pay the higher price.

The oil money that came into Saudi Arabia solved many problems, but it also created some. First of all, there were not enough Saudis with the skills necessary to work in the oil industry. Workers from other countries had to be brought in.

Riyadh, the capital of Saudi Arabia. Much of Saudi Arabia's money gained from the sale of oil has been spent on the development and expansion of its major cities.

These foreigners had different ideas and customs, and sometimes their ideas offended the Saudis.

Since there was so much oil money coming into the country, the prices of food, clothing, and other merchandise went up.
But the people who didn't work for the oil companies didn't get
any of the money. They couldn't pay the high prices, so they became even poorer. Also, many people who used to live in the
desert came to the cities to look for work with the oil companies.
But there weren't enough houses, schools, and hospitals for
them.

As time went on, the government began to solve some of
these problems. Much of the oil money was used to build schools,
roads, and other things the country needed. Plans were made to
develop new industries and to train the Saudis to work in them.
This development is still going on today. The Saudis are deter-
mined to use their oil to ensure a secure future for their country.

Islam: A Way of Life

There is really no way to understand the people of Saudi Arabia without understanding their religion, Islam. We have already read that Mohammed was born in what is now Saudi Arabia. The people of the Arabian Peninsula quickly converted to the new faith. Today, they still believe in the ideas that Mohammed taught long ago.

THE FIVE PILLARS OF FAITH

Muslims say that their religion has five important rules, called the Pillars of Faith. The first rule is that Muslims must believe in only one God. They must also believe that Mohammed is the messenger of God.

Second, all Muslims must pray five times a day. When

Muslims pray, they kneel down and touch their heads to the ground. No matter where they are in the world, they must face the direction of the holy city of Mecca while praying. And no matter what their nationality, they must pray in Arabic. In Muslim towns the people are reminded to pray by an official of the church called a *muezzin*. The muezzin stands on an outside balcony of the mosque and calls "God is Great" several times. He ends his praise of God by saying, "Prayer is better than sleep."

The third duty of every Muslim is to give money and help to the poor.

Fourth, during the month that is called *Ramadan* in Arabic, Muslims may not eat or drink until after sundown. Most Muslims prepare for this fast by having a big meal every morning before dawn. At the end of the day, they eat again.

The last rule is that every Muslim who is able to must visit Mecca at least once during his or her life. A religious visit to Mecca is called a *haji*. There is a special month called *Dhu-al-hijjah* set aside every year for these visits. During this month, Mecca and Medina fill with Muslims from all over the world. Each visitor to Mecca goes first to the Kaaba, a sacred black stone. There is a legend that says the Kaaba was built by Abraham, an important figure in the Old Testament. It is located in a small, square building in the middle of Mecca and is covered with black curtains that have religious sayings on them. Each Muslim circles the Kaaba seven times. Then the visitors go to the other holy places of their religion. Muslims who can afford to, make a trip to Mecca every year during Dhu-al-hijjah.

Muslims believe in life after death. They believe that if they follow these five rules and the other teachings of Mohammed they will be rewarded in heaven.

THE TEACHINGS
OF MOHAMMED

According to the beliefs of Islam, Mohammed was the most important messenger of God, but he was not the first. Throughout history God sent other messengers. People listened for a little while, and then forgot what they had been taught. Muslims believe that Adam, Noah, Moses, and Abraham were all messengers from God. They also believe that Jesus Christ was a messenger. They do not believe that Jesus was God. Muslims say that Mohammed was the last messenger — the world's last chance to learn about God.

Muslims believe the Word of God as told to Mohammed was written down in a book called the Koran. The Koran has 114 chapters, and is a little shorter than the New Testament of the Christian Bible. It is written in Arabic, and many Arabs think it is the most beautiful book ever written in that language.

Besides the Koran, Muslims have other books to tell them about the teachings of Mohammed. During his life he taught by speaking to his followers. Often people would ask his advice, and Mohammed would answer by giving general rules that Muslims could use. The ideas of Mohammed were collected by his follow-

If they are able, every Muslim is required to make a visit to Mecca at least once in his or her life. Once there, they gather around the Kaaba, the holiest of Muslim shrines.

(31)

ers and written down. They were called the *hadith*, which means tradition. The Koran and the hadith are the two basic guides that tell Muslims how to live a holy life.

RELIGION IN SAUDI ARABIAN LIFE

No one can be in Saudi Arabia for very long without seeing the influence of Islam on daily life. The Muslim holy day, for example, is Friday. And during the work week (Saturday to Wednesday) all work stops during prayer times.

There are other signs of the importance of Islam. Saudi Arabians are members of the group of Muslims called Wahhabis, the strictest sect of Muslims. The Wahhabis follow the teachings of Mohammed in the Koran and the hadith very carefully. So no smoking or drinking of alcohol is permitted in Saudi Arabia. Because the Koran forbids the worship of images, there are no paintings or statues of people. Advertisements can show a new product, but not a person using the product. Muslim churches are decorated with beautiful patterns of flowers, fruit, and letters. But there are no statues of Mohammed or pictures of God.

The influence of religion in Saudi Arabian life can also be seen in the role of women. Mohammed taught people that women should stay at home and obey their husbands. This rule is still very strictly followed in Saudi Arabia. Saudi women are separated from any men who are not close relatives. In front of strangers, they must wear a veil over their faces so that only their eyes show. They are not allowed to drive vehicles in the cities. They cannot go to coffee shops or parties with their husbands. If they go to any public places, they must go on "women only"

Thousands of Muslims camp outside Mecca during their pilgrimage to the holy city.

days. If they want to go to the zoo in Riyadh, for example, they must go on Thursdays and Saturdays. On the other days, only men are allowed.

Until recently, Saudi girls received no formal schooling. This is changing now, but there are still many more boys than girls in school. Those girls who do go to school must study separately from boys. In some Saudi colleges there is no separate building or female teacher available. In that case, the women watch their lesson on television rather than sit in a classroom with men. Few women work outside of the home, and those who do must remain separated from men. The only Saudi Arabian women who have a little more freedom are the Bedouin women who live in the desert. They do not have to wear a veil and are allowed to speak to men outside their own families.

Islam has also greatly influenced the government and laws of Saudi Arabia. The king is both head of the government and head of the church. The laws are based on the Koran and the hadith.

Customs and Arts

In trying to understand another country, there are many important factors to consider. The weather, the religion, and the government certainly influence the way people live. But there are also many small but important details that make up a lifestyle, such as the kind of food that is eaten, and the kind of art enjoyed.

FOOD

There are some things that Saudi Arabians eat that are enjoyed all over the world, such as dates, lamb, chicken, eggplant, and cheese. There are, however, a few dishes that might sound a little strange to foreigners. For example, the Saudis like the milk and meat of camels. But perhaps their strangest food of all would be locusts. Locusts are insects that live in great numbers in the Arabian desert, and are broiled or roasted by the Saudis as a special treat!

When guests are invited, Saudis prepare an enormous feast. A whole roasted sheep stuffed with almonds, chicken, and eggs might be served. Several side dishes of vegetables, rice, and sweets would also be cooked. Pork is never served, since it is forbidden by the Koran.

A Saudi meal today is eaten at a Western-style table complete with silverware. Long ago, the dishes of food were placed on the floor and the family sat around them on cushions. By custom, only the right hand was used when eating, and people ate with their fingers. Meat was broken off bit by bit, and vegetables were picked up with bread.

Guests in a Saudi house are treated like kings. A traditional custom, still followed by some Saudis, calls for the host to eat after his guests. This is to make sure the guests have had enough to eat. If only family members are present, men and women eat together. But if any strangers have been invited, the women have to eat separately. A guest has to be careful not to admire anything in his friend's house, because if he does, a Saudi custom says that the host has to give it to him.

Before and after meals, Saudi Arabians wash their hands with perfumed water. After they have finished eating, incense is burned to make the air smell sweet. Coffee is also served at the end of a meal. Green coffee beans are brought to the table and roasted in an open pot before being crushed into a fine powder. The powder is mixed with sugar and water and cooked until it is thick and syrupy. The coffee is served in small cups. The host will make sure that his guest's coffee cup is kept filled, until the guest stops him by putting a hand over the top of the cup.

NAMES

Family relationships are also very important to the Saudis. Within a family, people are called by their title, or position in the family. A cousin might be "son of my aunt" or "daughter of my aunt." Parents might be called "Father of Fatima" or "Mother of Ali," depending on the name of the oldest child. Children are called "ibn," which means "son of," or "bint," which means "daughter of." Saudi Arabians generally use only their father's name, but they can also take the names of their grandfather, great-grandfather, and as many other ancestors as they want. Ibn Saud, the name of the founder of modern Saudi Arabia, means "son of Saud." But he was only called that for short — his full name was King Abd al-Aziz ibn Abd al-Rahman al Faisal al Saud.

THE CALENDAR

Western and Muslim countries use two different methods of counting years. The western year 1978, for example, is the Muslim year 1398. This is because Westerners count years from the year fixed as the birth of Christ. According to the Western calendar, years are really counted "A.D.," which is an abbreviation of the words "in the year of Our Lord" in Latin. Muslims also count years from an important day in their religion — the flight in 622 A.D. of Mohammed from Mecca into Medina. That flight is called *hegira* in Arabic, so Muslim years are counted

"A.H." "A.H." is an abbreviation for the Arabic words that mean "in the year of the hegira." So the Western year 623 A.D. was the same as the Muslim year 1 A.H.

To make things even more complicated, the Muslim year is only 354 days long. This is 11 days less than the Western year. So a certain date, like the first of Ramadan, is 11 days earlier (according to the Western calendar) each year.

WRITING

Just as the Arabic language is so different from English, so is Arabic writing. There are 28 Arabic letters, compared to 26 in the English alphabet. These 28 letters are all consonants with vowels shown by small marks above and below. Arabic is written from right to left — the opposite of English. The writing is very beautiful, using curved, graceful strokes. Writing well is considered a fine art.

Written Arabic is also a link between Saudi Arabia and the other Arab countries. Over 100 million people from all over the world speak Arabic. But because of different dialects, people from different countries sometimes find it hard to understand each other. They often have slightly different ways of saying a word. Written Arabic, however, is the same everywhere.

PASTIMES

Like everything else, the pastimes enjoyed by Saudi Arabians have changed a lot in recent years. Saudis who live in large towns or cities can now watch television or listen to the radio. All radio and television stations are owned by the government, and many of the broadcasts are educational or religious. But Egyptian "soap operas" and popular music are also broadcast. And of course there are also newspapers, magazines, and movies in the cities of Saudi Arabia.

Basketball, soccer, and volleyball are popular sports with Saudi schoolchildren. The youngest children play some games that are familiar in many countries — tug of war, for example. Men go to coffee shops to have coffee with friends. Women stay mostly at home, but they also have social clubs where they can visit. Whole families can go to each other's homes, but men and women usually visit separately.

LITERATURE, MUSIC, AND ART

Saudi Arabia has never had a long literary heritage. This is largely because until recently very few people could read and write. However, the Saudis do have a great love of oral, or spoken, poetry. There are many beautiful examples of Arab poetry in history.

In the past, the poems were memorized by a professional reciter, a person who journeyed with a poet, listening to the poems. After a few years, the reciter had learned them by heart, and could say them out loud to an audience. Some of these poems describe the beauty of the desert or the courage of the nomad's animals. Others praised the poet's tribe or criticized another tribe. Still others talked of a poet's lost love. Even today, the Bedouins enjoy listening to these poems around the campfire at night.

Mohammed did not approve of music, although he did not forbid it in the Koran. For this reason there have not been great

Men enjoy coffee in an open-air coffee shop while
a woman in full veil passes on a street in Jidda.

Saudi composers or performers. Some music is, however, written and played in Saudi Arabia.

The Koran forbids making pictures or statues of people and animals, so Islamic artists have had to concentrate on other subjects. The most common designs are patterns of fruit, flowers, and letters. Muslim artists also use geometric forms, like squares, circles, and triangles, that are woven into rugs and painted or carved on walls. They are also baked into pottery.

Saudi Arabia Today

Saudi Arabian people today face a problem most people would enjoy having. They must decide what to do with all the money their oil has brought them. And there certainly is a lot of money. In 1977, the Saudi government reported that it had a trade surplus in the amount of almost 28,000,000,000 dollars. And there's still a lot more oil to sell.

How Saudi Arabia has handled this situation so far is very interesting. When money from the sale of oil started to come in, Saudi Arabia was one of the least developed countries in the world. Less than 10 percent of the people knew how to read and write. Many people were leading a nomadic lifestyle that had changed little for hundreds of years. Not many houses had running water, electricity, or indoor plumbing. There were few hospitals and schools, and no schools at all for girls. There were practically no industries, and agricultural methods were out-dated. Saudi Arabia had a lot of catching up to do.

A CHANGING LAND

The Saudis have made amazing progress so far. Education is a good example. In 1953 there were only 44,000 students in school in the whole country. Now, only 25 years later, there are 800,000. Before 1960 there were no girls at all in school. Now, about 200,000 Saudi girls are receiving an education. There are also many new schools for technical education, and several new colleges. All schools are owned by the government, and cost nothing for Saudis.

New hospitals have also been built. Fifty years ago there was almost no advanced medical care in Saudi Arabia, but now there are private hospitals and clinics in all major cities. The new King Faisal Specialist Hospital, located in Riyadh, is one of the most modern in the world. Medical care, like education, is free to the Saudis.

Transportation has grown rapidly as well. In 1960 there were only 1,000 miles (1,600 km) of paved roads in the country. Now there are over seven times as many, and the number is increasing every day. Cities on the coasts, such as Jidda, have improved their ports so that they can move goods in and out of the country more quickly. There is only one rail line in the country, but the Saudi Arabian airline, Saudia, now serves all the major cities. It also flies to many cities in Europe, and will soon fly to the United States.

Oil money is also helping to solve the great desert problem

of a lack of water. The Saudis used to rely on old-fashioned wells for their water. But now some factories have been built to take the salt out of seawater. New watering systems have been refined that enable Saudis to make farmland out of desert. They have even developed plans to tow icebergs from the South Pole to their country to provide more fresh water!

New office buildings, high-rise apartments, and hotels are being built in every major city. But there is still a great shortage of housing in Saudi Arabia. The government has had to make a rule that foreign companies have to bring ready-made houses for their employees.

INDUSTRY AND AGRICULTURE

Industry has grown too. Before the discovery and development of oil, Saudi Arabia's only industries were raising animals, fishing, agriculture, and taking care of visitors to Mecca. In recent years, however, the country has developed a great number of new industries.

The most important of these new industries is, of course, oil. First, the oil has to be taken from the ground and transported to the seacoast. Then it has to be loaded into huge ships and sent to other countries, where it is made into fuel, fertilizer, plastic, and other products. While Saudi Arabia used to export all its oil to other countries, the Saudis have now built the factories necessary to make these things themselves. Then they sell these finished products to other countries. Factories for the manufacture of many heavy materials, such as steel and cement, are also being built.

However, very few Saudis are employed in these new indus-

Until 1960, women were not allowed a formal education.

tries. This is partly because there are not enough Saudis with the proper training, so foreigners have to be hired to fill the jobs Saudis don't know how to do. But the government recently has taken steps to solve this problem by sending many young Saudi men to Europe and America for advanced education. And, in Saudi Arabia itself, new colleges have been built. More and more Saudis, for example, are studying at the College of Petroleum and Minerals. When they graduate they can take jobs now held by foreigners. Right now, however, the Saudis still need many workers from other countries. Today there are over two million foreigners working in Saudi Arabia.

Some of Saudi Arabia's old industries have remained relatively intact. Taking care of Muslim visitors is one of them. The two holiest cities of the Islam religion, Mecca and Medina, are in Saudi Arabia. If they are able to, Muslims must visit Mecca during a special month of the year. Most people visit Medina also. These visitors need hotels, food, and other services.

Another occupation remaining from the past is agriculture, the industry that employs the largest number of people in Saudi Arabia. Dates, wheat, barley, rice, corn, fruit, and coffee are grown. Camels, horses, donkeys, and sheep are raised. But because of the shortage of water, and the difficulty in growing crops, Saudi Arabia still has to import much of its food.

IMPORTANT CITIES

All these new industries have made Saudi Arabian cities grow very rapidly in the past few years. One of the most important cities in Saudi Arabia is Riyadh, the capital. Riyadh is located near the middle of the country, and is home for the king's residence and most government offices. It is a modern city with many hotels and restaurants. There is also a zoo, a football stadium, and several museums. The name Riyadh means "The Gardens" in Arabic. The city received its name because of the beautiful palm gardens that grow there.

Saudi Arabia's leading seaport is Jidda, located on the Red Sea. It is Saudi Arabia's most international city. Most foreign diplomats have offices in Jidda, and Muslims going to Mecca and Medina come to Jidda first. Most manufactured goods also enter Saudi Arabia by way of Jidda so the city has a busy airport and port. The city is called Jidda because it means grandmother in Arabic, and it is supposed to be the place where Eve, the first woman, is buried.

Dhahran, a city on the eastern coast, is the headquarters of the oil industry. The main offices of the Arabian American Oil Company (ARAMCO) are in Dhahran.

Mecca and Medina are in western Saudi Arabia. In Mecca is the Kaaba, Islam's most sacred shrine. Other important places in Mecca are the Great Mosque and the house where Mohammed was born. Mecca is so sacred that non-Muslims are not allowed in the city at all. A few years ago, foreign engineers were needed to help build a hotel in Mecca, but since they were not Muslims, they could not actually enter the city. They had to look at the building on closed-circuit television and direct the work from outside the city!

In Medina there is an important Muslim church called the Prophet's Mosque. The tombs of Mohammed and his daughter Fatima are also in Medina.

Above: Jidda harbor
Opposite: Saudi Arabia is a monarchy,
with King Khalid the head of state.

GOVERNMENT AND LAWS

Saudi Arabia is a monarchy, which means that it is ruled by a king. The king is the head of the government and also the head of the church. He is helped by a council made up of members of the royal family, religious leaders, and sheikhs of important tribes. The *ulama*, a group of religious leaders who help interpret the law, also gives advice to the king.

Saudi Arabia is divided into 18 provinces. The provinces have governors appointed by the king, and councils that advise the governors. Cities also have councils, and tribal leaders govern small towns. There is no voting or parliament in Saudi Arabia.

A decree issued by King Ibn Saud in 1926 stated that Saudi Arabia's laws would be based on the laws of Islam. Any rules Mohammed made in the Koran or the hadith are the law in Saudi Arabia. If there is anything not covered in the Koran or the hadith, the king issues a decree. Even traffic laws, for example, are made by the king.

Crimes are judged in religious courts. There are no juries, but people can appeal their cases to the king. Perhaps because punishments are severe, there is very little crime in Saudi Arabia. Thieves may have a hand cut off at the wrist. Someone who has committed a serious crime may be stoned to death or even beheaded.

A Leader in the Arab World

OIL POWER

All the countries of the world need oil to run their cars, machinery, and industries. The Saudis have the largest deposits of oil in the world. So their decisions about who buys oil and how much must be paid for it are very important.

In 1974, the Saudis raised the price of oil by 400 percent, and the other OPEC nations did the same. As the Saudis saw it, oil had been sold much too cheaply through the years and they were beginning to feel they were being cheated. They thought that the oil countries were selling oil to other nations at low prices while they had to buy back manufactured goods at high prices. This, said the Saudis, was unfair. They convinced the other

A field of oil tanks located at Ras Tanura on the Persian Gulf.

OPEC countries that they should make more money from their oil. So the OPEC countries announced to the world that the days of cheap energy were over.

This price increase caused problems in the industrialized countries of the world. Products made from oil cost more to make. The price of electricity and heating oil went up. Anything that had to be transported by cars or trucks cost more, since fuel was more expensive. In fact, since oil has so many uses, the price of almost everything rose sharply.

The higher prices forced some companies out of business, while others had to lay off thousands of workers. People had to get used to paying more for lights and heat in their homes.

Every country in the world that imported oil was now in trouble. For the first time they realized how powerful the OPEC nations were and how dependent they were on OPEC oil. The oil companies were powerful because they could raise the price of oil as high as they wanted. If the OPEC nations raised the price of oil too high, some countries would run out of money completely.

Little by little, the industrialized countries got used to paying more for their oil. Some learned to use less oil so that they didn't have to pay as much. But they always had to worry that the price of oil might rise higher than they could pay.

Since 1974, oil prices have not risen as sharply. Oddly enough, the Saudis have been an important influence in keeping the price down. While they were the ones who wanted to raise the price in the first place, the Saudis now have important reasons for wanting to keep the price low. They are afraid that if oil prices are too high, some countries might be ruined and would not be in a position to buy oil at all. They are also afraid that the people in these countries might overthrow their governments and become communists. Since communism as we know it in the world today does not promote religious freedom, the Saudis do not want this to happen. So they have tried to influence the other OPEC countries to keep the prices down. So far they have succeeded. But the OPEC nations still have the same power to raise prices, if they wish to use it. Every country in the world that depends on imported oil must face this fact.

SAUDI ARABIA AND ISRAEL

Most of the countries of the Middle East are Arab countries. The one exception, of course, is Israel. Israel is a Jewish nation located to the north of Saudi Arabia, on the Mediterranean Sea. Since it was founded in 1948, Israel and the Arab countries around it have fought four wars. Saudi Arabia, like all the countries of the Middle East, has been affected by these wars.

To understand the Middle East it is important to understand the Arab-Israeli problem. The land of Israel was originally called Palestine. In ancient times the Jews had lived in Palestine, although through the years it had been conquered many times. At one time it was part of the Arabian Empire, and many Arabs still live there.

At the end of World War I, Palestine was under the control of Great Britain. At that time, the Jewish people had no country of their own in the Middle East. The British government made a statement saying that someday they would give the Jews a homeland in Palestine.

At the end of World War II, Jews from all over the world began to move to Palestine. The Arabs of Palestine were at odds with the Jews, and so were the nearby Arab countries.

In 1948, Britain gave up its control of Palestine and the country was divided into three parts. One part went to the Jews and became the country of Israel. Another part went to the Arab country Jordan. Finally, a small section was given to Egypt. The Jews were happy with this settlement, but the Arabs were not. The Arabs who lived in the Jewish section of Palestine felt that their homeland had been stolen. War broke out immediately, and fighting occurred again in 1956, 1967, and 1973. Each time Israel won. But the Arab states of the Middle East have never accepted this situation. They feel that Arab land was stolen from them and given to the Jews.

Saudi Arabia wants very much to see the land of Israel returned to the Arabs. Although they have sent only a few troops to fight Israel, they have given money to Egypt and Jordan, two countries that have fought against Israel. They have also given money to the Palestine Liberation Organization (the PLO), an important group that is fighting for an independent Arab Palestine.

Saudi Arabia has used its "oil power" against Israel too. In 1973, some Arab countries, including Saudi Arabia, announced that they would send no more oil to countries that supported Israel. This caused an "energy crisis" in all the countries that depend on Arab oil. Without the imported oil, there was not enough fuel for cars, factories, and homes. The United States and the Netherlands, who are not as dependent on Saudi oil, continued to support Israel but some countries turned their support to the Arabs. In 1974, the Arabs lifted the ban and began to sell oil to any country again.

The Saudis have tried to hurt Israel in other ways. They have refused to buy from any country that does business with Israel. Since the Saudis have so much money to spend, supporting Israel becomes an important political and financial decision for many governments.

How the Middle East problem will finally be solved no one knows. But it seems likely that Saudi Arabia will continue to at least support other Arab countries in their fighting with Israel.

THE FUTURE

Oil is a natural resource that will eventually run out. The Saudis are already planning for life after this happens. No one knows exactly when that will be. Some experts say that the oil will last until the year 2018. But in 1976 alone, the Saudis discovered more oil than they sold. An official in charge of water complained that every time he drilled for water he found oil! But no matter how long it lasts, the oil supply won't last forever.

Saudi Arabia is trying to prepare for that day by investing money in industries in other countries. In their own country they are building more "non-oil" industries, as well as exploring their land for new minerals. The Saudis hope this will give them other sources of money after the oil runs out.

In the meantime, the government is trying to use the oil money to improve the quality of life in Saudi Arabia. The Saudis have drawn up a plan for their country's development over the next few years. Included in this plan are all the things they would like to build by the year 1980, such as new airports, schools, factories, roads, and ports.

Saudi Arabia is trying hard to accomplish everything in its five-year plan. If it succeeds, it will truly be a modern country by the year 1980. But that alone is not enough. The Saudis want to make progress, but only if they can maintain their traditional values at the same time.

In Saudi Arabia today, religion, family, and friendship are important, and the Saudis want to keep it that way. But can they? A lot changed in Saudi Arabia after oil was discovered. Some of these changes were in material objects, like hospitals and roads. But other changes were in ideas. Some of these ideas came from the foreigners who worked in the new industries, and some came from the Saudis themselves, as they learned from their new experiences.

Many of these ideas were beneficial for the country. Slavery, for example, was outlawed in Saudi Arabia in 1963. Education for women was begun in 1960.

Some of the changes in Saudi society, however, were not so beneficial. The crime rate rose when foreigners came into the country, and some of the traditional Saudi customs were no longer followed. Old people and orphans, for example, had always been taken care of by their families or tribes. But when people moved to the cities to work in the new industries, they were far away from their relatives and unable to care for them. So the government had to begin plans to take care of the needy.

The most important challenge facing Saudi Arabia is not building new roads or schools. The challenge is to take the best of the modern world while holding on to the best of their past traditions and customs. Only time will tell if the Saudis will be able to meet that challenge.

Books for Further Reading

Caldwell, John C. *Let's Visit the Middle East*. New York: John Day Company, revised edition, 1972.

Gordon, Eugene. *Saudi Arabia in Pictures*. New York: Sterling Publishing Company, 1974.

Lang, Andrew. *Arabian Nights*. New York: David McKay Company, 1946. (Tales from the time of the Arabian Empire.)

Lengyel, Emil. *Oil Countries of the Middle East*. New York: Franklin Watts, 1973.

Phillips, Ted. *Getting to Know Saudi Arabia*. New York: Coward, McCann, and Geoghegan, revised edition, 1971.

Raswan, Carl. *Drinkers of the Wind*. New York: Ariel Books, Farrar, Strauss and Cudahy, 1961. (A young boy lives with the nomadic Bedouins and helps them with their horses. Based on the real life experiences of the author.)

Index

(62)

About the Author

Presently a writer by profession,
Geraldine Woods taught grades five
through eight in a New York City
school for several years. She has
toured extensively through Europe,
and now spends most of her time in
New York with her husband and son.

This is her first book for Franklin Watts.